I'll never
forget
you

THIS BOOK BELONGS TO

_____

WEBSITE

USERNAME

PASSWORD

NOTES

WEBSITE

USERNAME

PASSWORD

NOTES

WEBSITE

USERNAME

PASSWORD

NOTES

WEBSITE

USERNAME

PASSWORD

NOTES

WEBSITE

USERNAME

PASSWORD

NOTES

WEBSITE

USERNAME

PASSWORD

NOTES

A

WEBSITE

USERNAME

PASSWORD

NOTES

WEBSITE

USERNAME

PASSWORD

NOTES

WEBSITE

USERNAME

PASSWORD

NOTES

WEBSITE

USERNAME

PASSWORD

NOTES

_____

WEBSITE

USERNAME

PASSWORD

NOTES

_____

WEBSITE

USERNAME

PASSWORD

NOTES

B

WEBSITE

USERNAME

PASSWORD

NOTES

WEBSITE

USERNAME

PASSWORD

NOTES

WEBSITE

USERNAME

PASSWORD

NOTES

WEBSITE

USERNAME

PASSWORD

NOTES

WEBSITE

USERNAME

PASSWORD

NOTES

WEBSITE

USERNAME

PASSWORD

NOTES

B

WEBSITE

USERNAME

PASSWORD

NOTES

WEBSITE

USERNAME

PASSWORD

NOTES

WEBSITE

USERNAME

PASSWORD

NOTES

WEBSITE

USERNAME

PASSWORD

NOTES

WEBSITE

USERNAME

PASSWORD

NOTES

WEBSITE

USERNAME

PASSWORD

NOTES

C

WEBSITE

USERNAME

PASSWORD

NOTES

WEBSITE

USERNAME

PASSWORD

NOTES

WEBSITE

USERNAME

PASSWORD

NOTES

WEBSITE

USERNAME

PASSWORD

NOTES

WEBSITE

USERNAME

PASSWORD

NOTES

WEBSITE

USERNAME

PASSWORD

NOTES

WEBSITE

USERNAME

PASSWORD

NOTES

WEBSITE

USERNAME

PASSWORD

NOTES

WEBSITE

USERNAME

PASSWORD

NOTES

WEBSITE

USERNAME

PASSWORD

NOTES

WEBSITE

USERNAME

PASSWORD

NOTES

WEBSITE

USERNAME

PASSWORD

NOTES

D

WEBSITE

USERNAME

PASSWORD

NOTES

WEBSITE

USERNAME

PASSWORD

NOTES

WEBSITE

USERNAME

PASSWORD

NOTES

WEBSITE

USERNAME

PASSWORD

NOTES

WEBSITE

USERNAME

PASSWORD

NOTES

WEBSITE

USERNAME

PASSWORD

NOTES

D

WEBSITE

USERNAME

PASSWORD

NOTES

WEBSITE

USERNAME

PASSWORD

NOTES

WEBSITE

USERNAME

PASSWORD

NOTES

WEBSITE

USERNAME

PASSWORD

NOTES

WEBSITE

USERNAME

PASSWORD

NOTES

WEBSITE

USERNAME

PASSWORD

NOTES

WEBSITE

USERNAME

PASSWORD

NOTES

WEBSITE

USERNAME

PASSWORD

NOTES

WEBSITE

USERNAME

PASSWORD

NOTES

WEBSITE

USERNAME

PASSWORD

NOTES

WEBSITE

USERNAME

PASSWORD

NOTES

WEBSITE

USERNAME

PASSWORD

NOTES

WEBSITE

USERNAME

PASSWORD

NOTES

WEBSITE

USERNAME

PASSWORD

NOTES

WEBSITE

USERNAME

PASSWORD

NOTES

WEBSITE

USERNAME

PASSWORD

NOTES

WEBSITE

USERNAME

PASSWORD

NOTES

WEBSITE

USERNAME

PASSWORD

NOTES

WEBSITE

USERNAME

PASSWORD

NOTES

WEBSITE

USERNAME

PASSWORD

NOTES

WEBSITE

USERNAME

PASSWORD

NOTES

WEBSITE

USERNAME

PASSWORD

NOTES

WEBSITE

USERNAME

PASSWORD

NOTES

WEBSITE

USERNAME

PASSWORD

NOTES

WEBSITE

USERNAME

PASSWORD

NOTES

WEBSITE

USERNAME

PASSWORD

NOTES

WEBSITE

USERNAME

PASSWORD

NOTES

WEBSITE

USERNAME

PASSWORD

NOTES

WEBSITE

USERNAME

PASSWORD

NOTES

WEBSITE

USERNAME

PASSWORD

NOTES

WEBSITE

USERNAME

PASSWORD

NOTES

WEBSITE

USERNAME

PASSWORD

NOTES

WEBSITE

USERNAME

PASSWORD

NOTES

WEBSITE

USERNAME

PASSWORD

NOTES

———————

WEBSITE

USERNAME

PASSWORD

NOTES

———————

WEBSITE

USERNAME

PASSWORD

NOTES

G

WEBSITE

USERNAME

PASSWORD

NOTES

WEBSITE

USERNAME

PASSWORD

NOTES

WEBSITE

USERNAME

PASSWORD

NOTES

WEBSITE

USERNAME

PASSWORD

NOTES

WEBSITE

USERNAME

PASSWORD

NOTES

WEBSITE

USERNAME

PASSWORD

NOTES

WEBSITE

USERNAME

PASSWORD

NOTES

WEBSITE

USERNAME

PASSWORD

NOTES

WEBSITE

USERNAME

PASSWORD

NOTES

WEBSITE

USERNAME

PASSWORD

NOTES

WEBSITE

USERNAME

PASSWORD

NOTES

WEBSITE

USERNAME

PASSWORD

NOTES

WEBSITE

USERNAME

PASSWORD

NOTES

WEBSITE

USERNAME

PASSWORD

NOTES

WEBSITE

USERNAME

PASSWORD

NOTES

WEBSITE

USERNAME

PASSWORD

NOTES

WEBSITE

USERNAME

PASSWORD

NOTES

WEBSITE

USERNAME

PASSWORD

NOTES

WEBSITE

USERNAME

PASSWORD

NOTES

WEBSITE

USERNAME

PASSWORD

NOTES

WEBSITE

USERNAME

PASSWORD

NOTES

WEBSITE

USERNAME

PASSWORD

NOTES

WEBSITE

USERNAME

PASSWORD

NOTES

WEBSITE

USERNAME

PASSWORD

NOTES

WEBSITE

USERNAME

PASSWORD

NOTES

WEBSITE

USERNAME

PASSWORD

NOTES

WEBSITE

USERNAME

PASSWORD

NOTES

WEBSITE

USERNAME

PASSWORD

NOTES

WEBSITE

USERNAME

PASSWORD

NOTES

WEBSITE

USERNAME

PASSWORD

NOTES

J

WEBSITE

USERNAME

PASSWORD

NOTES

WEBSITE

USERNAME

PASSWORD

NOTES

WEBSITE

USERNAME

PASSWORD

NOTES

WEBSITE

USERNAME

PASSWORD

NOTES

WEBSITE

USERNAME

PASSWORD

NOTES

WEBSITE

USERNAME

PASSWORD

NOTES

J

WEBSITE

USERNAME

PASSWORD

NOTES

WEBSITE

USERNAME

PASSWORD

NOTES

WEBSITE

USERNAME

PASSWORD

NOTES

WEBSITE

USERNAME

PASSWORD

NOTES

WEBSITE

USERNAME

PASSWORD

NOTES

WEBSITE

USERNAME

PASSWORD

NOTES

WEBSITE

USERNAME

PASSWORD

NOTES

WEBSITE

USERNAME

PASSWORD

NOTES

WEBSITE

USERNAME

PASSWORD

NOTES

WEBSITE

USERNAME

PASSWORD

NOTES

WEBSITE

USERNAME

PASSWORD

NOTES

WEBSITE

USERNAME

PASSWORD

NOTES

WEBSITE

USERNAME

PASSWORD

NOTES

WEBSITE

USERNAME

PASSWORD

NOTES

WEBSITE

USERNAME

PASSWORD

NOTES

WEBSITE

USERNAME

PASSWORD

NOTES

WEBSITE

USERNAME

PASSWORD

NOTES

WEBSITE

USERNAME

PASSWORD

NOTES

WEBSITE

USERNAME

PASSWORD

NOTES

WEBSITE

USERNAME

PASSWORD

NOTES

WEBSITE

USERNAME

PASSWORD

NOTES

WEBSITE

USERNAME

PASSWORD

NOTES

WEBSITE

USERNAME

PASSWORD

NOTES

WEBSITE

USERNAME

PASSWORD

NOTES

WEBSITE

USERNAME

PASSWORD

NOTES

WEBSITE

USERNAME

PASSWORD

NOTES

WEBSITE

USERNAME

PASSWORD

NOTES

WEBSITE

USERNAME

PASSWORD

NOTES

WEBSITE

USERNAME

PASSWORD

NOTES

WEBSITE

USERNAME

PASSWORD

NOTES

WEBSITE

USERNAME

PASSWORD

NOTES

WEBSITE

USERNAME

PASSWORD

NOTES

WEBSITE

USERNAME

PASSWORD

NOTES

WEBSITE

USERNAME

PASSWORD

NOTES

WEBSITE

USERNAME

PASSWORD

NOTES

WEBSITE

USERNAME

PASSWORD

NOTES

WEBSITE

USERNAME

PASSWORD

NOTES

WEBSITE

USERNAME

PASSWORD

NOTES

WEBSITE

USERNAME

PASSWORD

NOTES

WEBSITE

USERNAME

PASSWORD

NOTES

WEBSITE

USERNAME

PASSWORD

NOTES

WEBSITE

USERNAME

PASSWORD

NOTES

WEBSITE

USERNAME

PASSWORD

NOTES

WEBSITE

USERNAME

PASSWORD

NOTES

WEBSITE

USERNAME

PASSWORD

NOTES

WEBSITE

USERNAME

PASSWORD

NOTES

WEBSITE

USERNAME

PASSWORD

NOTES

WEBSITE

USERNAME

PASSWORD

NOTES

N

WEBSITE

USERNAME

PASSWORD

NOTES

WEBSITE

USERNAME

PASSWORD

NOTES

WEBSITE

USERNAME

PASSWORD

NOTES

WEBSITE

USERNAME

PASSWORD

NOTES

———

WEBSITE

USERNAME

PASSWORD

NOTES

———

WEBSITE

USERNAME

PASSWORD

NOTES

WEBSITE

USERNAME

PASSWORD

NOTES

WEBSITE

USERNAME

PASSWORD

NOTES

WEBSITE

USERNAME

PASSWORD

NOTES

WEBSITE

USERNAME

PASSWORD

NOTES

WEBSITE

USERNAME

PASSWORD

NOTES

WEBSITE

USERNAME

PASSWORD

NOTES

WEBSITE

USERNAME

PASSWORD

NOTES

WEBSITE

USERNAME

PASSWORD

NOTES

WEBSITE

USERNAME

PASSWORD

NOTES

WEBSITE

USERNAME

PASSWORD

NOTES

WEBSITE

USERNAME

PASSWORD

NOTES

WEBSITE

USERNAME

PASSWORD

NOTES

P

WEBSITE

USERNAME

PASSWORD

NOTES

WEBSITE

USERNAME

PASSWORD

NOTES

WEBSITE

USERNAME

PASSWORD

NOTES

P

WEBSITE

USERNAME

PASSWORD

NOTES

WEBSITE

USERNAME

PASSWORD

NOTES

WEBSITE

USERNAME

PASSWORD

NOTES

WEBSITE

USERNAME

PASSWORD

NOTES

WEBSITE

USERNAME

PASSWORD

NOTES

WEBSITE

USERNAME

PASSWORD

NOTES

P

WEBSITE

USERNAME

PASSWORD

NOTES

WEBSITE

USERNAME

PASSWORD

NOTES

WEBSITE

USERNAME

PASSWORD

NOTES

WEBSITE

USERNAME

PASSWORD

NOTES

WEBSITE

USERNAME

PASSWORD

NOTES

WEBSITE

USERNAME

PASSWORD

NOTES

WEBSITE

USERNAME

PASSWORD

NOTES

WEBSITE

USERNAME

PASSWORD

NOTES

WEBSITE

USERNAME

PASSWORD

NOTES

WEBSITE

USERNAME

PASSWORD

NOTES

WEBSITE

USERNAME

PASSWORD

NOTES

WEBSITE

USERNAME

PASSWORD

NOTES

WEBSITE

USERNAME

PASSWORD

NOTES

———

WEBSITE

USERNAME

PASSWORD

NOTES

———

WEBSITE

USERNAME

PASSWORD

NOTES

R

WEBSITE

USERNAME

PASSWORD

NOTES

WEBSITE

USERNAME

PASSWORD

NOTES

WEBSITE

USERNAME

PASSWORD

NOTES

WEBSITE

USERNAME

PASSWORD

NOTES

WEBSITE

USERNAME

PASSWORD

NOTES

WEBSITE

USERNAME

PASSWORD

NOTES

WEBSITE

USERNAME

PASSWORD

NOTES

WEBSITE

USERNAME

PASSWORD

NOTES

WEBSITE

USERNAME

PASSWORD

NOTES

R

WEBSITE

USERNAME

PASSWORD

NOTES

WEBSITE

USERNAME

PASSWORD

NOTES

WEBSITE

USERNAME

PASSWORD

NOTES

S

WEBSITE

USERNAME

PASSWORD

NOTES

WEBSITE

USERNAME

PASSWORD

NOTES

WEBSITE

USERNAME

PASSWORD

NOTES

S

WEBSITE

USERNAME

PASSWORD

NOTES

WEBSITE

USERNAME

PASSWORD

NOTES

WEBSITE

USERNAME

PASSWORD

NOTES

S

WEBSITE

USERNAME

PASSWORD

NOTES

WEBSITE

USERNAME

PASSWORD

NOTES

WEBSITE

USERNAME

PASSWORD

NOTES

WEBSITE

USERNAME

PASSWORD

NOTES

WEBSITE

USERNAME

PASSWORD

NOTES

WEBSITE

USERNAME

PASSWORD

NOTES

WEBSITE

USERNAME

PASSWORD

NOTES

WEBSITE

USERNAME

PASSWORD

NOTES

WEBSITE

USERNAME

PASSWORD

NOTES

WEBSITE

USERNAME

PASSWORD

NOTES

WEBSITE

USERNAME

PASSWORD

NOTES

WEBSITE

USERNAME

PASSWORD

NOTES

WEBSITE

USERNAME

PASSWORD

NOTES

WEBSITE

USERNAME

PASSWORD

NOTES

WEBSITE

USERNAME

PASSWORD

NOTES

WEBSITE

USERNAME

PASSWORD

NOTES

WEBSITE

USERNAME

PASSWORD

NOTES

WEBSITE

USERNAME

PASSWORD

NOTES

WEBSITE

USERNAME

PASSWORD

NOTES

WEBSITE

USERNAME

PASSWORD

NOTES

WEBSITE

USERNAME

PASSWORD

NOTES

WEBSITE

USERNAME

PASSWORD

NOTES

WEBSITE

USERNAME

PASSWORD

NOTES

WEBSITE

USERNAME

PASSWORD

NOTES

WEBSITE

USERNAME

PASSWORD

NOTES

WEBSITE

USERNAME

PASSWORD

NOTES

WEBSITE

USERNAME

PASSWORD

NOTES

WEBSITE

USERNAME

PASSWORD

NOTES

WEBSITE

USERNAME

PASSWORD

NOTES

WEBSITE

USERNAME

PASSWORD

NOTES

WEBSITE

USERNAME

PASSWORD

NOTES

WEBSITE

USERNAME

PASSWORD

NOTES

WEBSITE

USERNAME

PASSWORD

NOTES

WEBSITE

USERNAME

PASSWORD

NOTES

WEBSITE

USERNAME

PASSWORD

NOTES

WEBSITE

USERNAME

PASSWORD

NOTES

WEBSITE

USERNAME

PASSWORD

NOTES

WEBSITE

USERNAME

PASSWORD

NOTES

WEBSITE

USERNAME

PASSWORD

NOTES

WEBSITE

USERNAME

PASSWORD

NOTES

WEBSITE

USERNAME

PASSWORD

NOTES

WEBSITE

USERNAME

PASSWORD

NOTES

WEBSITE

USERNAME

PASSWORD

NOTES

WEBSITE

USERNAME

PASSWORD

NOTES

WEBSITE

USERNAME

PASSWORD

NOTES

WEBSITE

USERNAME

PASSWORD

NOTES

WEBSITE

USERNAME

PASSWORD

NOTES

WEBSITE

USERNAME

PASSWORD

NOTES

WEBSITE

USERNAME

PASSWORD

NOTES

WEBSITE

USERNAME

PASSWORD

NOTES

WEBSITE

USERNAME

PASSWORD

NOTES

WEBSITE

USERNAME

PASSWORD

NOTES

WEBSITE

USERNAME

PASSWORD

NOTES

WEBSITE

USERNAME

PASSWORD

NOTES

WEBSITE

USERNAME

PASSWORD

NOTES

WEBSITE

USERNAME

PASSWORD

NOTES

WEBSITE

USERNAME

PASSWORD

NOTES

WEBSITE

USERNAME

PASSWORD

NOTES

———————

WEBSITE

USERNAME

PASSWORD

NOTES

———————

WEBSITE

USERNAME

PASSWORD

NOTES

WEBSITE

USERNAME

PASSWORD

NOTES

WEBSITE

USERNAME

PASSWORD

NOTES

WEBSITE

USERNAME

PASSWORD

NOTES

WEBSITE

USERNAME

PASSWORD

NOTES

WEBSITE

USERNAME

PASSWORD

NOTES

WEBSITE

USERNAME

PASSWORD

NOTES

WEBSITE

USERNAME

PASSWORD

NOTES

WEBSITE

USERNAME

PASSWORD

NOTES

WEBSITE

USERNAME

PASSWORD

NOTES

WEBSITE

USERNAME

PASSWORD

NOTES

WEBSITE

USERNAME

PASSWORD

NOTES

WEBSITE

USERNAME

PASSWORD

NOTES

WEBSITE

USERNAME

PASSWORD

NOTES

WEBSITE

USERNAME

PASSWORD

NOTES

WEBSITE

USERNAME

PASSWORD

NOTES

WEBSITE

USERNAME

PASSWORD

NOTES

WEBSITE

USERNAME

PASSWORD

NOTES

WEBSITE

USERNAME

PASSWORD

NOTES

Z

WEBSITE

USERNAME

PASSWORD

NOTES

WEBSITE

USERNAME

PASSWORD

NOTES

WEBSITE

USERNAME

PASSWORD

NOTES

WEBSITE

USERNAME

PASSWORD

NOTES

WEBSITE

USERNAME

PASSWORD

NOTES

WEBSITE

USERNAME

PASSWORD

NOTES

Z

WEBSITE

USERNAME

PASSWORD

NOTES

WEBSITE

USERNAME

PASSWORD

NOTES

WEBSITE

USERNAME

PASSWORD

NOTES

WEBSITE

USERNAME

PASSWORD

NOTES

WEBSITE

USERNAME

PASSWORD

NOTES

WEBSITE

USERNAME

PASSWORD

NOTES

Made in the USA
Monee, IL
07 July 2026